SIMPLE & EFFECTIVE

WAYS TO

SAVE YOUR MARRIAGE

Copyright © 2022 by Carrie C. Remer All Rights Reserved.No part of this book may be used or reproduced by any means, graphic,electronic, or mechanical, including photocopying, recording, taping, or by any information storage retrieval system without the written permission of the publisher.

Introduction

Almost every wedding begins with a big party. Each couple has many goals and dreams for their future life together, along with their family and friends. But staying married happily is by no means an easy journey. And many couples decide not to finish the voyage, as today's divorce rates all too clearly show.

It would be simple to attribute our high rate of divorce on neglecting to spend enough time together, allowing resentment and hatred to fester, and failing to maintain open channels of communication. You can learn how to enhance these and numerous other elements of your relationship through a variety of books, articles, and seminars. This book is one of such helpful resources for resuscitating and saving your marriage from collapsing.

CHAPTER 1

How to Save Your Marriage

Following a short period into marriage, a few contentions between couples might emerge and wedded life might become upsetting. How might you come to realize that your marriage is in conflict? There are a few reasons answerable for upset wedded life, for example, alcohol misuse, trouble with kids, monetary issues, a circumstance when both parties are not trustworthy, significant life changing events and issues

 that something is the matter with your wedded life, don't simply figure out how to save your marriage, quickly swing into action. You attempt to figure out the issues and take on certain characteristics to save your marriage and to stop the separation that is likely coming. There are in every case expectations and ways of settling the issues your marriage. The contentions in wedded life might be because of pride or a few misconceptions.

Subsequently, to keep up with solid connections, you ought to surrender self image and ought to show a drive to determine the issues in your wedded life. Self-evaluation is a vital stage to save your marriage. You ought to have the option to ponder your missteps and foster an improvement in your way of behaving. Try not to do those things that can hurt your spouse.

There are a few valuable choices for the issue of how to save a marriage. To be a decent spouse, you ought to have an ability to pay attention to your spouse and grasp him/her. You ought to have the option to try to avoid panicking and talk through the issue(s). At the point when your partner is conversing with you, you ought to take responsibility of all issues raised and explain all questions.

Great conversation is a vital variable for fostering the solid connections. You ought to impart all issues and sentiments to your partner. Mainly, you ought to completely trust your partner and never be envious about his/her own advancement.

Your approach towards your relationship and wedded life ought to be positive. Whenever there are a few issues or frictions, recall the cheerful moments that you had spent together and attempt to reignite these moments. At the point when there are a few issues, don't get upset or frenzy, simply keep things level headed. At the point when you burst in anger during contentions, you by and large will quite often say and do the things that you really didn't mean.

One of the most incredible ways of saving a marriage is to make long haul plans with your spouse. Make a few arrangements to go for a vacation or spend time at a great cookout spot. A few tentative arrangements that are made together may assist with increasing the closeness. It will guarantee that your spouse is generally there for you.

Your general character and cleanliness likewise significantly affect your wedded life. Consequently, attempt to be generally respectable, courteous and tidy. The most effective methods to save a Marriage ought not be a risky issue by any means.

Attempt some of above techniques and make your wedded life worry free and a wonderful one.

CHAPTER 2

Saving the Marriage for the sake of your Children

Getting separated is an exceptionally straightforward process, however it leaves a high effect on private and day to day life of an individual. The individual going through this cycle might face part of torment and stress and lose the individual as well as social security.

It is an incredibly upsetting experience particularly for the kids of separating from parents, despite their sex and age. They might get intellectually upset and their future might get ruined. Therefore, saving the marriage for the sake of the children is frequently encouraged.

As the separation influences the economical status of an individual, it could become hard for a single parent to take good care of a kid or kids. Since, separation or divorce isn't socially acceptable in certain nations or cultures, the kid(s) might feel humiliated in the general public. There might be a few issues in profound holding of youngsters and guardians. The children of divorcees could encounter a feeling of extreme outrage, uncertainty and depression.

The results of separation influence pretty much every part of the kids' lives, for example, feelings and cognitive abilities, mental downturn and the parent to child relationship. The youngsters might feel vulnerable and alone because of frustration which might prompt some medical conditions like sleeplessness.

There might be a few horrendous changes in kids' way of behaving, for example, alcohol misuse, illicit drug use, savagery or the endeavors to take their own life. Other conduct issues include anxiousness, school issues or backward ways of behaving like bed-wetting or unusual use of solace things like bedcovers or stuffed toys. Consequently, prior to your choice of action, figure out certain ways of saving the marriage for the sake of your kids.

When you conclude that you ought to save the marriage for the kids, you ought take action immediately. You can start by figuring out the issues in your marriage and ways of settling them. At the point when you come to "about the issues", both of you need to take endeavors to tackle them and save the marriage.

There must be able to properly communicate your sentiments and to pay attention to and grasp that of your spouse. You might take the assistance of your family or companions and get a guidance from them. If for any reason this isn't adequate, you can go for marriage counseling and seminars which might assist you with grasping your individual difference and recommend a few ways to solve them.

CHAPTER 3

5 Simple but Effective Ways to Save Your Marriage

Marriage is one of the happiest and memorable moments of our lives. It is a union of not only two individuals, but also of two different backgrounds and cultures. After a cheerful start of married life, there might be a possibility or beginning of some conflicts. These may be due to some misunderstandings, ego or other personal problems. Sometimes the bitterness in the relation crosses the tolerance level that the couples think of getting separated.

However, a divorce affects the personal and social lives of both the partners. You will be surprised to know that your marriage problems can be resolved.

Here are 5 ways to save a marriage that can be effectively implemented in your married life.

Be Realistic

The first step to resolve the marriage problems is to agree that they exist. You should be honest with yourself, should be able to identify the differences in your relationships and try to improve them. If your try to go away from the issues, they will never be solved. Accept the situation as it is and be prepared for the challenges which may lie ahead.

Communicate

It is said that you cannot fight the enemy that you cannot see. This philosophy is absolutely true in case of marriages. If you feel that your spouse has changed the way of interaction, then find out the reasons behind it. The best solution is to start a conversation with your spouse and give him several opportunities to 'open up'. Keep your ears and mind open for the subtle hints from his conversation.

Reignite Your Love

Saving your marriage is not merely solving the problems. Reigniting your love for each other is one of the effective 5 ways to save a marriage. You can express your passion for your partner with special dates or surprises. Remember the most romantic times you spent together and recreate them with an addition of a unique approach.

Create Time

Give some time for each other to share the feelings. The purpose is to grab the attention of your partner and make your relationships healthy with natural attraction. If you are successful in developing the passion for each other, then other problems can be immediately solved.

There may be many obstacles when you are trying to fix the relationships. It might be difficult for you to communicate with your husband or you may be facing outside pressures from the family which may prevent you to focus on your goals. Even after facing these barriers, you should be persistent on your aims. If one approach fails, you can try another approach that may work. You should be able to handle the conflicts safely.

Right Counsel

One of the important steps among 5 ways to save a marriage is to seek the right advice from your friends and family. You should try to get an expert advice from counseling sessions or books before you take any major decision. A wise advice can save your marriage, while bad advice may ruin it.

Knowing about this 5 ways to save a marriage, you would be able to resolve the problems if any in your marriage and live a happy married life.

CHAPTER 4

Save Your Marriage And Avoid Divorce

Save My MarriageToday, many marriages are found to be ending in divorce. Marriage is a start of relation, while divorce is an end. After passing of few days or months of married, life, some conflicts and bitterness may get started. Sometimes, the couple began to think about the divorce.

However, divorce changes social trends and causes adverse effects for the both the partners. Hence, it is always recommended to save marriage stop divorce.

Marriage has a great importance in the life of every human being as it gives personal and social stability and it is also necessary to satisfy your emotional and physical needs. It may be essential to get the prestigious social status as living a single or getting separated is not accepted by the society in some countries.

It is not easy for a man or a woman to live alone whole life. After divorce, the individual may have to face physical, psychological and economical problems. The family life of the person is totally collapsed. Divorce also can cause sexual deprivation.

Separation or divorce of the parents affects a lot to the children. It may give rise to psychological problems which can affect the tender minds of children as they need both the parents equally. The children may get mentally and physically disturbed and feel insecure due to which their future may get spoiled. Looking towards these effects, you should strive to save marriage stop divorce.

It is not easy to keep the relationships alive, for that, you have to take some efforts. If you strongly wish to save marriage stop divorce, you should try to improve yourself. Some possible factors that can affect your relationships are the broken trust, boredom, infidelity, poor communication, addictive behavior, emotional abuse, absence of sex and affection and lack of appreciation.

Once you know about the reasons, you should try to find out the options to solve them. The main reason for the divorce is a lack of understanding and compromises. Hence, you should give away your ego to maintain the healthy relationships and should take an initiative to resolve the problems in your married life.

Self-assessment is a very important step to save marriage stop divorce which includes thinking about your mistakes. If you want to be a good partner, you should have a capacity to listen to your partner and understand him/her for which you need a good communication skill. You should be able to keep calm and talk through the problem. When your partner is talking with you, you should ask the related questions and clarify the queries.

If you both are not able to solve problems in your married life, you can consult your family or friends and seek an advice from them. You may realize your mistakes after talking with them and can try to correct them. If you don't feel it satisfactory, you can try for marriage counseling. You may go to counselor's office and find the solutions to save marriage, stop divorce.

Counseling can help the couples to improve their communication skills, to uncover some other problems or issues, find out the differences and understand the troubles. You can also go for a trial separation which gives the couple enough time for to think about their differences, their mistakes, problems in their married life and ways to resolve them.

CHAPTER 5

Can Seperation Save A Marriage

Save My MarriageSometimes, married life may become extremely stressful and the couple may find it miserable to live together. When this happens, some couples wish to have a trial separation which may help to work through the difference between both the partners. In some cases, separation is prohibited by cultural or religious rules and they prefer to live apart though legally remaining married. The question is that can separation save a marriage and does it really work?

There two ways of marriage separation, either informal separation or legal separation. Generally, informal separation is what you both agree by a mutual understanding. There is a formal division of the property, arrangements about possession of cars, credit cards and bank accounts. A legal, formal separation is more complicated, permanent and expensive. People undergoing the process of legal separation go through time, pain and expense.

Generally, separation is not the first step to save a marriage. Many couples first try to participate in marital counseling which may help to work through the differences. Some couples seek out an advice from the friends, family or religious leaders. Many people are successful in resolving their marital problems after participating in couple retreats or marriage seminars.

Along with these options or after trying these options, the couples choose a trial separation. Now, you will wonder can separation save a marriage; is it an appropriate way to save a marriage? Yes, it may be helpful as it gives an opportunity to both the partners to experience the feelings of being separated before taking any final decision. The major advantage of trial separation is that it is reversible.

During the period of trial separation, you may go through marital counseling, think over it and then take the final decision. This separation period gives you ample time to think about your differences, your mistakes, problems in your married life and ways to resolve them.

An absence of daily bickering and conflicts may be an effective answer to the question can separation save a marriage. Due to a lack of proximity, there is absolutely no chance for conflicts. Both the partners get enough time to think over their marital problems. Most of the marital problems originate from fear, ego or stubbornness. Resolution is possible as long as one partner wishes to keep trying.

The main purpose of trial separation is to develop the skills of resolving the problems before moving back together and working on improving the relationships. For a couple, a planned separation can be a good time to think, to analyze, to reflect, to calm down and cool off. It helps to make thoughtful decisions and thus work to save a marriage.

In some cases, separation may be unplanned and there may be no plans for marriage counseling, no tentative time-line for separation and no guidelines agreed about seeing others. Hence, before you think about separation, talk with each other about the individual goals of separation. Both should be ready for seeking individual and joint counseling during the separation period.

The answer to the question 'can separation save a marriage' lies within the person himself/herself;

you need to realize how important your spouse is in your life and how life may be without him/her.

CHAPTER 6

Can You Save A Marriage Alone?

The unfortunate question asked by the plenty of people. Today, many couples are facing some or the other problems in their married life. The first few years of married life are cheerful, but after some years, problems may arise due to conflicts along with bitterness and some misunderstanding. Generally, nobody directly thinks of breaking a marriage as it is hurting to both the partners. Every couple tries to find out some ways to resolve the problems in their married life and save a marriage.

Once you agree that there are some problems in your married life, you may need to think and find the reasons why. Off-course, it will be just like a one-way traffic and it is quiet difficult that you alone should try to improve your relations. Your partner should equally respond to your efforts to save your marriage. However, you must make some efforts to find out the problems in your married life and develop some qualities within you to maintain better relationships.

The first step you may need to take in order to save your marriage is to bring back the spark in your relationship again. It is very important to spend time with each other. You may use this time to relax and enjoy in each other's company and recall the moments that you had spent together.

This may help to do away with the misunderstandings and resolve the conflict if any. You should show deep love for your partner and make him/her feel how much you need him/her. Love is an important bridge in a married life that may keep the couple bound together. You may send a romantic message to your partner or arrange for the romantic outings.

Self-assessment is a very important solution to the question can you save a marriage alone. You should be able to realize your mistakes and develop ways to improve your behavior. Avoid the things that may hurt your partner. The conflicts in married life may be due to ego or some misunderstandings. Hence, you should give away your ego and should take an initiative to resolve the problems in your married life. You should be ready for the compromises it demands.

Good communication is a very important factor for developing healthy relationships. You should share all your problems, expectations and feelings with your partner. Communication is not limited to just talking with others, but you should be able to listen to your partner and understand him/ her. The most important thing is that you should fully trust your partner and have faith in your relationship.

Keeping the marital relations alive is very challenging. Always remember that during the course of time, both the partners may change. It is also very important to learn how to deal with these changes. Off-course, it requires efforts and cooperation from both sides. But, you can take an initiative from your side and start to work on the problems in married life.

If you are still wondering, can you save a marriage alone, and then the answer is yes! You can save a marriage alone if you are ready to put in some efforts first.

CHAPTER 7

Using Love Poems to Save A Relationship

Love is said to be one of the greatest feelings in the world which makes the people bound together. Love acts as an important bridge in a married life that may keep the couple attached together. Whenever you feel that your marriage is in crisis, you get worried about it and look of the options to save your marriage. There are numerous ways that you can try for improving your marital relationships. One of the most effective options is to keep a romantic approach.

If you feel that your marriage is in trouble, try to find out the reasons behind that. It may be because of broken trust, infidelity, poor communication, lack of appreciation, addictive behavior, absence of sex and no affection. Absence of love may result in misunderstanding, bitterness and conflicts. Hence, when you think about how to save the marriage, you should first try to create love for each other.

There are different ways to express your love for your partner such as special dates or surprises. Remember the most romantic times you spent together and recreate them with an addition of a unique approach. Romance is the chord which makes the heart beat strong. You may apply some romantic ideas such as to send romantic message, prepare romantic meal, watch a romantic movie together or offer a romantic gift. Among the romantic ideas, writing love poems to save a relationship can be very effective.

The love poems contribute a lot to express your love for your partner. Sometimes you want to express your passion, but you may be feeling shy or awkward, at that time love poems work. If there is some bitterness in your relation due to conflicts or misunderstandings, you can take help of love poems to save a relationship. The elegant and emotional words written in the love poems help to control the situation.

You can directly write or send love poems through SMS. When your partner will read these poems, he/she will realize your affection and immediately give away the bitterness which will help to resolve all conflicts.

You may face a problem about how to write love poems to save a relationship. When you are writing the love poems for your partner, you need not follow the general rules of poetry. Use of a single stanza may be enough to express your feelings. The main purpose of writing the poem is to express your passion for your partner.

You may describe about beauty, good nature and attitude of your partner in romantic words. You may also write about how much you love your partner, how much you need him/her and how your life is incomplete without your partner. It will impart a positive effect on your marriage life and help to improve your relationships.

If you are not able to write the poems, you can take help of numerous poetry books which are available in the market. You can take some lines from the romantic poems written by famous romantic poets and send them to your partner. The purpose is to grab an attention of your partner and make your relationships healthy with natural attraction.

Use of love poems to save a relationship is a wonderful way to express love for each other which may help to solve other problems as well.

www.ingramcontent.com/pod-product-compliance
Lightning Source LLC
Chambersburg PA
CBHW020136180726
47992CB00023B/3210